Robin,

I appreciate the gift of your friendship. Here's to many more years!

Rose

D1551104

THE GIFT OF
friendship

THE GIFT OF
friendship

sophie bevan

RYLAND
PETERS
& SMALL

LONDON NEW YORK

Designer Pamela Daniels

Senior Editor Clare Double

Picture Research Claire Hector

Production Patricia Harrington

Art Director Gabriella Le Grazie

Publishing Director Alison Starling

First published in the
United States in 2004 by
Ryland Peters & Small, Inc.
519 Broadway
5th Floor
New York NY 10012
www.rylandpeters.com

10 9 8 7 6 5 4 3 2 1

Text, design, and photographs
© Ryland Peters & Small 2004

ISBN 1 84172 733 4

Printed and bound in China

contents

kindness

Let us be grateful to people who make us happy, they are the charming gardeners who make our souls blossom.

MARCEL PROUST (1871–1922)

One can pay back the loan of gold, but one dies forever in debt to those who are kind.

MALAYAN PROVERB

Shared joy is double joy, and shared sorrow is half-sorrow.

SWEDISH PROVERB

Oh, the comfort, the inexpressible comfort of feeling safe with a person, having neither to weigh thoughts nor measure words, but pouring them all out, just as they are, chaff and grain together, certain that a faithful hand will take and sift them, keep what is worth keeping, and with a breath of kindness blow the rest away.

DINAH CRAIK (1826–1887)

A kind word is like
a spring day.

RUSSIAN PROVERB

One who does not envy but is a compassionate friend to all ... such a devotee is very dear to Me.

BHAGAVAD GITA 12.13–14

The language of Friendship is not words, but meanings. It is an intelligence above language.

HENRY DAVID THOREAU (1817–1862)

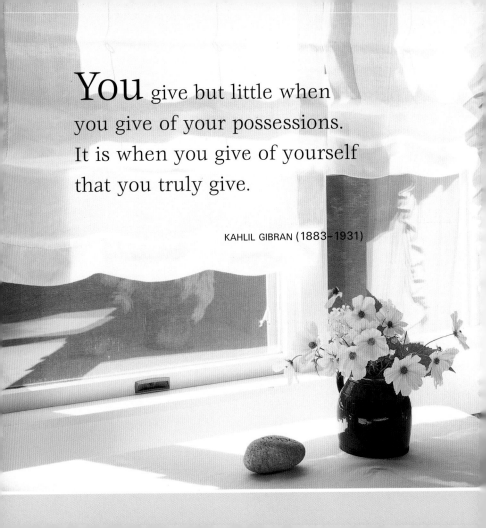

You give but little when you give of your possessions.
It is when you give of yourself that you truly give.

KAHLIL GIBRAN (1883–1931)

The greatest good
you can do for another
is not just to share
your riches but to
reveal to him his own.

BENJAMIN DISRAELI (1804–1881)

I felt it shelter to
speak to you.

EMILY DICKINSON (1830–1886)

Friendship is certainly the finest balm for the pangs of disappointed love.

JANE AUSTEN (1775–1817)

Wherever there is a human being, there is an opportunity for a kindness.

SENECA (1ST CENTURY)

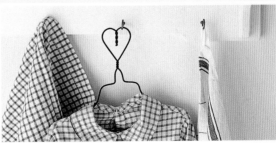

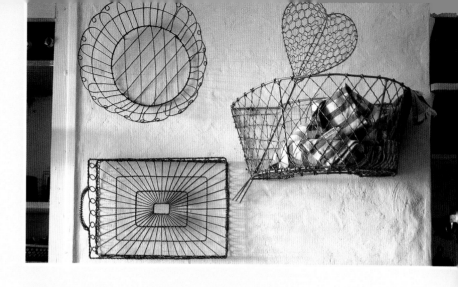

That best portion of a good man's life,
His little, nameless, unremembered acts
Of kindness and of love.

WILLIAM WORDSWORTH (1770–1850),

LINES COMPOSED A FEW MILES ABOVE TINTERN ABBEY

The only reward of virtue
is virtue; the only way to have
a friend is to be one.

RALPH WALDO EMERSON (1803–1882), *ESSAYS*

The more we come out
and do good to others, the more
our hearts will be purified,
and God will be in them.

SWAMI VIVEKANANDA (1863–1902)

If instead of a gem,
or even a flower, we
should cast the
gift of a loving
thought into
the heart of
a friend,
that would
be giving as
the angels give.

GEORGE MACDONALD (1824–1905)

Love is blind; friendship closes its eyes.

ANONYMOUS

Kindness

is the language which the deaf can hear and the blind can see.

MARK TWAIN (1835–1910)

In true friendship, in which I am expert, I give myself to my friend more than I draw him to me. I not only like doing him good better than having him do me good, but also would rather have him do good to himself than to me; he does me most good when he does himself good.

MICHEL DE MONTAIGNE (1533–1592)

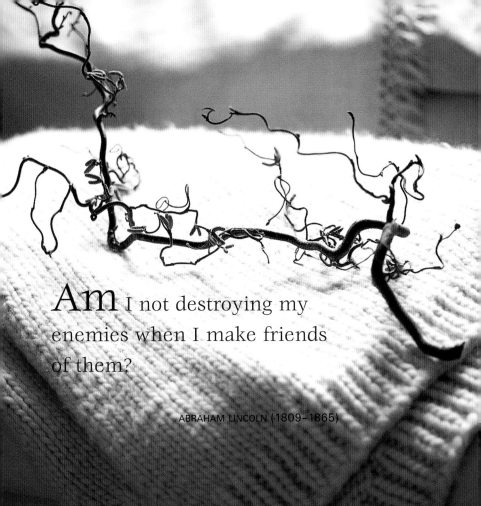

Am I not destroying my enemies when I make friends of them?

ABRAHAM LINCOLN (1809–1865)

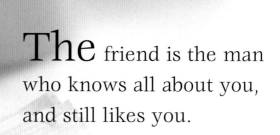

The friend is the man
who knows all about you,
and still likes you.

ELBERT HUBBARD (1856–1915)

Be good to parents, and to kindred, and to orphans, and to the poor, and to a neighbor, whether kinsman or newcomer, and to a fellow traveler, and to the wayfarer, and to the slaves whom your right hands hold; verily, God loveth not the proud.

QUR'AN SURA IV 9–10

loyalty

Friendship

is one mind in two
bodies.

MENCIUS (372–278 B.C.)

True friends

stab you in the front.

OSCAR WILDE (1854–1900)

Only your real
friends will tell you when
your face is dirty.

SICILIAN PROVERB

If I do vow a friendship,
I'll perform it
To the last article.

WILLIAM SHAKESPEARE (1564–1616), *OTHELLO*

But of all plagues,
good Heaven, thy
wrath can send,
Save me, oh, save me,
from the candid
friend.

GEORGE CANNING (1770–1827),

NEW MORALITY

We have been friends together
  together
In sunshine and in shade.

CAROLINE SHERIDAN NORTON (1808–1877),
WE HAVE BEEN FRIENDS

Love is

like the wild
rose-briar;
Friendship like
the holly-tree.
The holly is dark when
the rose-briar blooms,
But which will bloom
most constantly?

EMILY BRONTË (1818–1848),

LOVE AND FRIENDSHIP

The wing of friendship never moults a feather!

CHARLES DICKENS (1812–1870), *THE OLD CURIOSITY SHOP*

It is not so much our friends' help that helps us, as the confidence of their help when in need.

EPICURUS (341–270 B.C.)

True friendship destroys envy.

FRANÇOIS, DUC DE LA ROCHEFOUCAULD (1613–1680)

Friendship is the only cement that will ever hold the world together.

WOODROW WILSON (1856–1924)

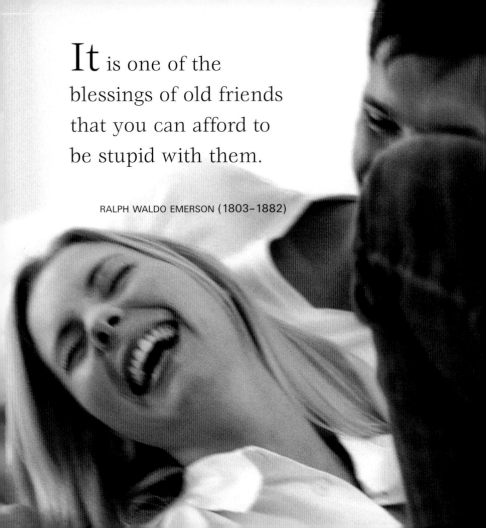

It is one of the blessings of old friends that you can afford to be stupid with them.

RALPH WALDO EMERSON (1803–1882)

Oh, go and ask this river
 running to the east
If it can travel farther than
 a friend's love!

LI BAI (701–762), *PARTING AT A WINE SHOP IN NANJING*

'Tis a great confidence in a
friend to tell him your faults;
greater to tell him his.

BENJAMIN FRANKLIN (1706–1790)

Few delights can equal the mere presence of one whom we trust utterly.

GEORGE MACDONALD (1824–1905)

Never explain— your friends do not need it and your enemies will not believe you anyhow.

ELBERT HUBBARD (1856–1915)

The holy passion of friendship is of so sweet and steady and loyal and enduring a nature that it will last through a whole lifetime, if not asked to lend money.

MARK TWAIN (1835–1910)

I always felt that the great high privilege, relief, and comfort of friendship was that one had to explain nothing.

KATHERINE MANSFIELD (1888–1923)

The most I can do for my friend is simply be his friend.

HENRY DAVID THOREAU (1817–1862)

A true friend unbosoms freely, advises justly, assists readily, adventures boldly, takes all patiently, defends courageously, and continues a friend unchangeably.

WILLIAM PENN (1644–1718)

Tell me who is your friend and I'll tell you who you are.

RUSSIAN PROVERB

I don't need a friend who changes
when I change and who nods when I
nod; my shadow does that much better.

PLUTARCH (C.46–C.125 A.D.)

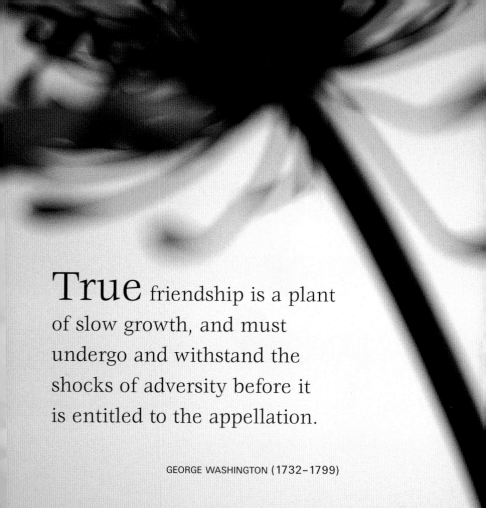

True friendship is a plant of slow growth, and must undergo and withstand the shocks of adversity before it is entitled to the appellation.

GEORGE WASHINGTON (1732–1799)

nurture

Hold a true friend with both your hands.

NIGERIAN PROVERB

Yes'm, old friends is always best, 'less you can catch a new one that's fit to make an old one out of.

SARAH ORNE JEWETT (1849–1909)

Ah, how good it feels! The hand of an old friend.

HENRY WADSWORTH LONGFELLOW
(1807–1882)

I shall think of you in a floating cloud;
So in the sunset think of me.

LI BAI (701–762), *A FAREWELL TO A FRIEND*

The stag cries even
In the mountains' farthest depths.

KOTAI KOGU NO TAYŪ TOSHINARI (12TH CENTURY)

Life without a friend is death without a witness.

But if the while
I think on thee,
dear friend,
All losses are restored
and sorrows end.

No road is long with good company.

TURKISH PROVERB

The greatest sweetener of human life is Friendship. To raise this to the highest pitch of enjoyment, is a secret which but few discover.

JOSEPH ADDISON (1672–1719)

Friendship is a serious affection; the most sublime of all affections, because it is founded on principle, and cemented by time.

MARY WOLLSTONECRAFT (1759–1797)

nurture

Another friend,
another door; another foe,
another wall.

CHINESE PROVERB

Friendship, mysterious
cement of the soul!
Sweet'ner of Life, and solder
of Society!

ROBERT BURNS (1759–1796)

I had three chairs in my house;
one for solitude, two for
friendship, three for society.

HENRY DAVID THOREAU (1817–1862), *WALDEN*

Forsake not an old friend; for the new is not comparable to him; a new friend is as new wine; when it is old, thou shalt drink it with pleasure.

THE BIBLE, ECCLESIASTICUS 9:10

Ceremony is the smoke of friendship.

CHINESE PROVERB

Since there is nothing so well worth having as friends, never lose a chance to make them.

FRANCESCO GUICCIARDINI (1483–1540)

"Stay" is a charming word in a friend's vocabulary.

LOUISA MAY ALCOTT (1832–1888)

Friendship,
like the immortality of the soul,
is too good to be believed.

RALPH WALDO EMERSON (1803–1882)

A friend is a gift you give yourself.

ROBERT LOUIS STEVENSON (1850–1894)

nurture

I have friends in overalls whose friendship I would not swap for the favor of the kings of the world.

THOMAS EDISON (1847–1931)

We cannot live only for ourselves. A thousand fibers connect us with our fellow men.

HERMAN MELVILLE (1819–1891)

Mighty proud I am that I am able to have a spare bed for my friends.

SAMUEL PEPYS (1633–1703)

photography credits

Key: a = above, b = below, r = right, l = left

Caroline Arber 28; Jan Baldwin 60; Carolyn Barber 61l; David Brittain 9l; Peter Cassidy 40; Vanessa Davies 29; Christopher Drake 15, 16r, 42; Dan Duchars 1, 9r, 13l, 21, 61r; Daniel Farmer 34; Craig Fordham 39; Catherine Gratwicke 32l, 64 Agnès Emery's house in Brussels, tiles and African-inspired drawer handles from Emery & Cie; Sandra Lane 8; Emma Lee 6, 12; Tom Leighton endpapers, 2–3, 7, 30, 54; James Merrell 16l, 23, 38a, 44, 46; Thomas Stewart 49; Debi Treloar 24, 31, 38b, 45; Chris Tubbs 11, 17, 50, 51a Daniel Jasiak's home near Biarritz, 51b Moens Dairyhouse in Dorset owned by Marston Properties Ltd (+ 44 20 7736 7133), 53, 55, 56–57 & 62–63 Daniel Jasiak's home near Biarritz; Simon Upton 14; Alan Williams 58 the Arbuthnott family's house near Cirencester designed by Nicholas Arbuthnott, fabrics designed by Vanessa Arbuthnott (www.vanessaarbuthnott.co.uk), 59; Polly Wreford 4–5, 13r, 18–19, 20, 33, 47, 48–49; Francesca Yorke 26, 32r, 36.

business credits

Nicholas Arbuthnott
Arbuthnott Ladenbury Architects
Architects & Urban Designers
15 Gosditch Street
Cirencester GL7 2AG

Agnès Emery
Emery & Cie
Noir D'Ivoire
Rue de l'Hôpital 25–29
1000 Bruxelles
+ 32 2 513 58 92
fax + 32 2 513 39 70
Moroccan tiles, concrete floor tiles, selected paints